GOD OF THE VALLEY

Mary Cervantes
God of the Valley

Published by Spines
ISBN 979-8-89691-666-6

GOD OF THE VALLEY

A STORY OF TRIUMPH OVER TRAGEDY

MARY CERVANTES

CONTENTS

Preface   ix
A letter from my mother to me   xiii

Chapter 1   1
Lucky Seven

Chapter 2   5
A brush with death

Chapter 3   10
On the seventh day

Chapter 4   13
An overwhelming sorrow

Chapter 5   16
Was I to blame?

Chapter 6   20
Welcome, Leah Rose

Chapter 7   26
Adam

Chapter 8   30
Bobby

Chapter 9   34
Rosa

Chapter 10   37
Joe

Chapter 11   45
Christina

Chapter 12   48
Steve

Chapter 13   52
Oscar

Life is a remarkable gift for all, but for God's children there is One who is with us, who will bear our griefs and carry our sorrows. In our most desperate hours, when we feel loneliness is unbearable, He hears our cry, knows our desolate hearts and He cares for us and comforts us. In our most vulnerable moments, He picks us up and holds us close. He shines His gracious light upon us in our darkest hour. No matter what obstacles we face or pain we endure, He is there, for He promised to never leave us nor forsake us. I will always honor Him and recognize that He is the answer to all my needs. He has promised to renew my spirit and make all things new. I developed an interest in writing when I was 12. My English teacher inspired me because she always admired and encouraged my creative writing. I had a natural desire to write because I found it is the best way to express my feelings and ideas. I let my mind explore a broad array of horizons where there are no limits. It's been my dream to write a book about the dramatic events of my life. I desire to tell the world my story, and in this way relive all those moments again. I thank God that I can finally make the dream of writing my story come true, knowing that my family is still with me. Tragedies endured and tears shed have made me stronger.

I could have never imagined where my treacherous journey through life would lead me. The many times I found myself at an end, not seeing a light at the end of the tunnel, I would cling to my heavenly Father and ask Him to guide me. Without His love and continual guidance, I would not be here to tell my story about my family—most of them gone now. I have often asked, Why Lord? Why have I been left behind to travel life's road alone? But in my heart, I know God has a plan for my life, and I am not alone because He travels with me down life's road. Only He knows the way, and I must follow Him. Job 23:10 says, But He knows the way that I take when He has tested me. I will come forth as gold (NIV).

I have often walked with Him through the valley of the shadow of death and I have found that He is the God of the Valley. Only God knows why I have survived this long, and as I pray for His guidance, I trust Him to lead me at last to perfect peace and joy in His house forever.

Mary Cervantes

2 Corinthians 4:8-10

We are hard pressed on every side, yet not crushed;
    we are perplexed, but not in despair;
    persecuted, but not forsaken;
    struck down, but not destroyed,
    always carrying about in the body
    the dying of the Lord Jesus
    that the life Jesus also
    may be manifested in our body.

A LETTER FROM MY MOTHER TO ME

In return yesterday that you saw me on the bus, you made me feel so good.

But I also saw love and mercy for me, your mother.

I love you and want to help you and your children with all my heart.

Please Mary pray for Adam as much as you can, so his seizures can go away.

Praying in silence helps prayers, it never hurt anybody.

God bless you. You have holy powers.

You were my seventh child. I wanted you to be born because

I loved when you were inside of me.

I saw something beautiful in you. I saw the holy virgin Mary in you.

You were born different, that is the reason I named you Mary.

Your personality is good, that is why so many people love you.

You are a very beautiful woman.

1

LUCKY SEVEN

My mother gave birth to six boys and then she had "Lucky Seven"—that's me. Mother called me that because I was her seventh child, I was born at seven o'clock in the evening, and I was a *girl*. I also had rich godparents —Robert Salas and his wife, who adored me. They owned a popular salon and had twins: a boy and a girl who were teenagers, when I came along. Mother said I was the only child in the family who had everything I wanted because of my wealthy godparents. They threw a big party to welcome me home.

My real name is Mary and I was born in the milehigh city of Denver, Colorado. My parents moved our family to San Antonio, Texas, when I was five years old. I remember that we rode a train from Denver, and it would have been a grand adventure except we couldn't take my big orange cat. We left him behind, and I cried and cried.

Mother finally convinced me that my cat had made it to Hollywood and was now the famous Morris, the cat. She said he was very happy because he was rich and famous. She showed me the commercial and sure enough, Morris did look like my cat. Mother didn't deceive me maliciously, it was the only thing that comforted me and stopped my mournful crying. I was proud of my cat for becoming famous.

I remember visiting my grandmother's house. She was my dad's mother. I also saw my grandfather who lay sick in a bed in the living room. My grandmother was tending to him. He looked sad and serious and one day later, he died, so I never got to know him. I was told that he was my father's father and that his name was Catarino Cervantes, Jr.

Mother made me and my brothers kneel and she taught us to pray. She taught us the Our Father. She said we would all go to the funeral home to see our grandfather, and we all needed to pray. At the funeral home, my brothers were scared to go to the front and pray. But I went down and prayed what my mother taught me the night before. I was sad and I understood very little of what it was all about. They said my grandfather was cousin to Emilio Zapata. He was very respected, and there were a lot of people at his funeral. Mother said Grandfather was very strict and no one dared disrespect him. He was a man of few words. With just one look, his children and his grandchildren knew exactly what he meant and what he expected of them.

We were very poor as we grew up, but my dad and mom always provided food, shelter, and the necessities. Mother often said in Spanish, "Where one eats, everyone eats." "She was always in the kitchen making tortillas and the most delicious food I have ever eaten. In spite of the fact that there were so many of us, Mother knew exactly what to cook in order to feed us all.

I especially remember one Christmas when I was six, and we lived in the projects. It was cheap housing and all we could afford. Father worked, while Mother stayed at home and cared for the nine of us.

On this particular Christmas, I had gone to a store with my

mother, along with two cousins, Rosalie and Maria. As we stood in a line waiting to see Santa Claus, my cousins were being mean to me, pushing and shoving me back and forth. I remember feeling very cold, and suddenly I fell down and went into a convulsion. Mother saw my skinny little body fall to the floor, and she rushed to my side. She later told me that she was terrified and lost a shoe as she ran to help me.

An ambulance came, and I woke up in the hospital. My arms were tied down, and tears were streaming down my cheeks. I asked my mother what was going on. She told me I had a convulsion and one of my pupils had moved, making one eye cross, but the doctors had operated on my eye and repaired it. She explained that my arms were tied, so I could not reach up and touch my eyes and damage the work the doctors had done. Her explanation didn't keep me from being sad. I was too young to fully understand what had happened and why it had happened to me.

When I was sent from the surgical suite to a room, there was another little girl in the room. She was all bandaged, but on her bed there were balloons, cards, stuffed animals and flowers. It looked magical to me. I had never seen anything so beautiful.

Mother told me the little girl had been burned over most of her body. I felt sorry for the little girl's burns, but I was so amazed by all her gifts that I thought she was the luckiest little girl in the whole world. She was loved by so many people and had all those wonderful things. I knew I would never have that many toys or nice dolls.

In spite of her lovely things, the little girl cried out in pain every time the doctors came to check her. I began to realize that the gifts couldn't stop her pain and I felt genuinely sad for her. Somehow my eye surgery wasn't so bad after all when compared to my roommate's pain from the terrible burns. I was also too young to realize how traumatic this had been for my mother whose small daughter had such a scary experience at Christmas, when children expect to experience wonder and excitement, not convulsions and eye surgery. But my mother was always so strong, calm and collected, that it never occurred to me to think about how she felt.

The next day Mother brought me a present. I was almost too excited to open it. I wanted the anticipation to last. When I finally opened the present, I found two small dolls. They were dark skinned, and my mother explained that they were all she could find at the gift shop.

I loved them at first sight and was overjoyed. I hugged my mom and kissed my dolls again and again. I told Mom how happy she had made me. At that moment, all was right with the world and I felt that life was precious.

When I finally went home, all my brothers and my sister were happy to see me. I had missed them more than I realized. I went back to school with a patch on one eye, and I had to wear it every day. I was in the first grade, and my classmates had a lot of fun at my expense, laughing at my eye patch and making fun of it and calling me names. I began to fight with my classmates because they made me so miserable and self-conscious.

After one particularly hard day, I told Mother that I was not going to school anymore wearing that patch. My parents talked, and they agreed to let me stay home. A year later I went back to school without the eye patch. My teacher was kind, and she was a good teacher who taught me well. I caught up quickly and was moved on to the second grade.

2

A BRUSH WITH DEATH

My mother was a homemaker, always either in the kitchen cooking or cleaning the house. She was an unusually strong and courageous woman, firm and decisive in all her ways. She managed to keep nine children well disciplined: my seven brothers, me, and Christine, my younger sister. Mom was mostly serious, but sometimes I could catch her off guard and make her laugh uncontrollably. It was a delightful sound, and it thrilled me to be able to fill her heart with laughter. After my mother's death I found a letter she wrote to me about the joy I had given her. My eyes overflowed with tears at the poignant memories.

Mother made it a daily chore to think of others. She often took clothing, blankets, and food to the homeless people under the bridge downtown. She told me many stories of how poverty played a role in her life. Her mother had credit at a corner store, so Mom and her sister would buy cold cuts and bread on Grandma's credit and feed her childhood friends after school. She would get a scolding when Grandma came home, but she couldn't resist being generous, even as a child.

My father, on the other hand, was an alcoholic. He worked

in a laundry and dry-cleaning plant. Most days after work, he went out drinking and came home drunk and beat my mother. My oldest brother Joe would stand in front of all of us when Dad attempted to beat us too. Sometimes Joe got a beating while trying to protect the rest of us.

After twenty-five years of this abuse, Mother decided she would not take it any more. She threatened to leave my father if he didn't get help with his drinking problem. Dad was afraid of losing her and his family, so he checked himself in at a rehabilitation unit at the State Hospital. He was there about six months, and I remember going with my mother to visit him. She took food to him and anything else he needed. She was always there to give him moral support. I also remember the other people who were there. They all looked crazy to me. I was scared, and I didn't understand what it was all about. I only knew it was supposed to make my dad stop drinking and beating my mother.

Dad finally came home, but even though he didn't drink any more, he was still violent toward our mother. Mother was a beautiful woman with light skin, long jet-black hair, and brown eyes. But she was a little plump. After all, she had conceived and birthed nine children and lost two others. But my dad was very jealous and could always find an excuse to be angry and violent.

Although Mom had never worked outside the home, she was smart and she found a job at a nursing home. Then she divorced my dad. In the coming years, life became even more difficult for Mom, and she would endure many tragedies. I regret to say, I was probably the first of her children to break our mom's heart. On August 20, 1977, at the age of twelve, I took all my mom's sleeping pills.

The day before I took the pills, a friend from school invited me to go with her to the amusement park Playland Park, on Broadway Avenue. Rosemary said her mother would take us and bring us home. My mother gave me permission to go.

Rosemary had two brothers: Albert and Mike, who both worked at Playland Park. Albert operated the fun house and Mike operated the roller coaster. Albert had a crush on me. He had asked Rosemary to take me by the fun house. When we arrived, Albert put someone else in charge of the fun house and went through it with me and Rosemary.

The fun house was a ride that wandered around in a maze of mirrors. We laughed and laughed, and had a wonderful time. We especially liked the three mirrors—one made you look tall and skinny, another made you short and fat, and the third made you very small. Albert found a way to lose his sister, so we were all alone. Albert was charismatic, a tall, handsome, charming guy with light skin and green eyes, but he was much older than me, probably about 19. He told me I was very mature for my age. He said he liked me a lot. We talked and talked and before I knew it, it was ten o'clock in the evening. This was when Rosemary's mom was supposed to pick us up, so we hurried to the designated meeting place, but her mom did not show up.

Finally, at eleven o'clock, I told Rosemary, I should call home because my mom would be very upset. There was a pay phone at the entrance of the park. I tried to call, but the line was busy. I didn't know what to do but wait. Finally, at midnight, I called the operator and asked her to break into the conversation at my house and tell whoever was on the phone that this was an emergency call. The operator tried, but my brother Steve was on the phone with his girlfriend Angie, and he refused to get off. Shortly after that, Rosemary's mother arrived. A flat tire had delayed her, but I knew I was going to be in big trouble; the next day I would surely get a beating from my mom for causing her so much worry.

When I finally got home everyone was asleep. The next day, my thirteen-year-old brother Jesse became very sick. Mom had to take him to the hospital where the doctor diagnosed Jesse with diabetes and told him he needed insulin. Mom was busy with Jesse all day, and my late night was not discussed. I was left at home with three of my brothers: Catarino, 15; Steve, 17; and Ricky, 20; to worry and brood about the consequences of my late adventure until my mother could find time to deal with it. My young preteen mind built it into a huge problem with dire consequences.

This is when I took all my mom's sleeping pills and then lay down on the living room sofa. My brothers thought I was just tired and sleeping off my late night, but suddenly I went into convulsions that wouldn't stop. They were coming one after another, so my brother Ricky took charge and called an ambulance. The ambulance took me to the nearest hospital, the downtown Metropolitan Hospital. Ricky said he almost crashed his car on the way to the downtown hospital to be with me.

Meanwhile, Rosemary had arrived at my house with a letter from her mother explaining everything about the night before, but by that time, it was too late and the paramedics were loading me into the ambulance.

When I arrived at the Metropolitan Hospital, they said they did not have the proper equipment to treat me. Then the emergency room attendants asked about my mother and Stevie explained that she was with my brother Jesse at another hospital. So they transported me to the Santa Rosa Children's Hospital because they had the lifesaving equipment that would be needed.

I was in a coma for six days, and I can remember the twelve years of my life flashing before me like a video as I slept. While I was in the coma, I could hear everyone talking and crying: my parents, all my brothers, my grandmother. I had not realized how much I was loved and it was an exhilarating experience.

3

ON THE SEVENTH DAY

The doctors told my parents to prepare for my funeral. I had been in a coma for six days and was not expected to come out of it. My mother did not want to tell my grandmother because she did not want to worry her, but it seemed hopeless, and she would soon have to know. So, on the seventh day of my coma, Mother broke down and called my grandmother.

Upon hearing the news, my grandmother immediately came to the hospital. She walked up to my bed, and I vividly remember her saying to me in Spanish: "Granddaughter, you have all your life ahead of you. You are only twelve years old. Someday you will get married and have children of your own. You *have* to live!" My grandmother demanded that I come back to my family and live.

Miraculously, as if in response to her demand, I woke up from the coma. I had a breathing tube coming out of my mouth, IVs in both arms, my hands were tied to the bedrails and there were machines attached to both legs.

The nurses asked if I wanted to see my mother. I shook my head. No, because I was ashamed and still a little scared about coming home so late. The nurses wanted to know why I didn't want to see my mother, but I kept silent. I had all kinds of confusing thoughts, but I *was* happy to be alive. Being in the coma made me realize how much everyone loved me. I knew it was God who had kept me alive.

On August 25, 1977, I was released from the hospital. I went to church frequently. It was a Baptist church, and I could feel God's presence. I was sorry for what I had done, not only to myself, but to my family. I felt great shame.

I remembered that Albert had come to the hospital when I was in the coma. He cried when he saw me, and I felt his tears on my face when he kissed my forehead. He told me goodbye and left a cross on my pillow. I had hurt many people. Albert went into the military soon after. He wrote to me many times, but my family did not let me see the letters.

Later, when Albert came home on leave, he came by to visit me. He asked if I had received his letters, and I said "What letters?" Later, I asked Mom about them and she gave them to me. Albert said he thought about me a lot while he was away. I knew that Albert really cared for me, but his age was a big factor at this point in my life.

My family was protective of me, especially after my foolish attempt to take my own life. My brother Steve said that after the coma I seemed different. He insisted that I was not the same. He felt that I had lost my innocence. I'm sure it was guilt and shame that made me somber.

My brother Joe also had a few conversations with me. He told me if I had wanted to kill myself, I should have done it right, in a way that would have succeeded. I told him I was wrong to have done what I did. I told him I now realized it was a sin against God, and I felt remorse. I tried to explain this to Joe, but he argued with me. At times, he just sat and stared at me. I think he may have felt that he wasn't there for me.

I had heard rumors from my other brothers that he had

beat up on Albert because he thought he was responsible for my suicide attempt. When he realized it wasn't Albert's fault, he even allowed Albert's visit while I was in a coma, but the cloud of suicide was still hanging over our family.

4

AN OVERWHELMING SORROW

The last time I saw Joe alive was the morning of September 4, 1977. Before I left for church that morning, I was in the kitchen getting some water from the refrigerator. Joe's room was next to the kitchen and it had no door. I happened to glance into his room and saw Joe tossing and turning in his bed like he couldn't sleep. I was worried about my brother and thought maybe I should stay home. At that very moment I heard the church van honking for me. The van took me to church every Sunday and brought me back afterward, so I ran out the door.

At church, after the Mass, our teachers put tables outside so we could all have punch and cookies. After church, I was sitting in a chair facing the freeway when I heard the wail of an ambulance. My heart began to pump fast. Somehow, I just knew it was for my brother Joe. When I got home, my brother Catarino was sitting on the sofa in the living room with a worried look on his face. I walked straight toward Joe's room, but Catarino stopped me. He said I couldn't go in there. I sat down and began to cry. I wanted to know what happened to my brother, yet I already knew. I felt at that precise moment that Joe had died.

I walked out on the front porch crying hysterically, and within minutes, cars began to pull up in front of our house. Then my father was walking toward me and my brother was trying to hold him back, saying, "No, don't tell Mary," but no one had to tell me anything; everyone was crying. My father continued to walk toward me and the terrible words I did not want to hear came out of his mouth: "Your brother shot himself in the head this morning and he is dead."

My mother tried to be strong for me, but I could see the pain in her eyes. My brother Steve was supposed to stand in his girlfriend's debut, but he canceled it. Instead of a happy occasion, we had to prepare for a funeral for Joe. Life would never be the same for my family.

Later, when I walked inside the funeral home, I couldn't believe my beloved brother was dead. Once I got close enough to touch him, I knew it was true: my big brother was dead. I started crying and screaming. I could not control myself. My mother and father took me back to the Santa Rosa Hospital to get help in controlling me. The hospital brought a Catholic priest to talk to me and console me. He told me my brother was with God now. But I kept saying, "No! My brother is alive. Just yesterday we talked." If I just denied it, maybe it wouldn't be true. The doctor gave me a sedative to help me sleep and my parents took me home. I didn't wake up until the next morning. When I did wake up, I knew it was true —Joe was gone. I sank into a depression.

My family was not the same after Joe died. I couldn't understand why my brothers and my parents kept asking me crazy questions like: What did your brother say when he talked to you? You were the last one to talk to him, what did he say? Did you know he might do this?

I was not sure it meant anything, but he did say something strange, so I told them: He said he was going to die and then mother and Adam will die. I asked him why he said that, and he said because that's the way things are gonna be. He told me that he was going to die, but I didn't know he meant by his own hand.

Joe had been very depressed and I didn't know how to help him. I did tell him not to say those things and to trust in God. I loved Joe more than anyone. He was my oldest brother, and He always looked out for me. My other brothers picked on me, but Joe would never pick on me. He and I were very close, now he was gone. He had shot himself at the age of 23. The day before he died, he had only spent time with me. I tried hard to remember everything he said that day. What were his last words? He wrote a suicide note that read: I love you all, Joe B. Cervantes.

Two years after Joe's suicide, I could feel that my family blamed me for it. After all, he took his life about a month after I had attempted to take mine. It was as if they thought I had given him the idea. Everyone was so proud of Joe and missed him so badly, I guess they needed someone to blame. I even blamed myself for not staying home that morning. Maybe I could have stopped him.

Joe had been a smart young man with tremendous talent in many areas. He was a good artist and had worked at other trades as well. He went to a Catholic school, then graduated from Fox Tech High School. Our father was very hard on him. When Joe worked, he took all his money, and if he came home drunk, he beat him. Father came home drunk regularly and wasn't a good example for his sons, but he held them to a different standard. That's the main reason Joe had joined the Army right after graduation. He served in the Airborne Infantry. He was stationed at Fort Polk, Louisiana, where he met an Indian girl named Glenda Myer.

Glenda got pregnant and had a baby girl that Joe named Rosie after our mother. Glenda was wild, so Joe ended up babysitting while Glenda went out drinking. Joe loved his little girl. The day before he died, he said it was her birthday. He knew he could never raise her because he had no love for Glenda. I told him if he tried hard enough, he could fight for her. I could see him thinking about that and I began to wonder if depression about this situation contributed to his decision to end his life.

After we buried Joe, the one thing that did not change was the regular beatings my father inflicted on our mother and whoever else might irritate him. A big change was taking place in my mother, and it was one reason why I was sure that she at least blamed me for my brother's death. She became very depressed and started to drink alcohol. She even attempted suicide herself. One night when she had been drinking, she swallowed a bunch of her pills. She told me what she had done, and I immediately called an ambulance. She was taken to the hospital and her stomach was pumped. Her depression was better after that, but violence took its place. It was obvious that she resented me because Joe was gone. When she drank, she became violent toward me screaming and throwing pots and pans at me. I was now 14 years old and I had a boyfriend who was 15 years old —Freddie, my brother Jesse's friend. One night my mother was drinking at a bar down the street on Main Avenue and Freddie and I waited outside the bar until she came out, so we could walk her home. When we got home, she became angry and violent toward me. She started throwing things at me, so Freddie insisted that I run away with him that night. I was scared, but I too was tired of my mother's abuse.

Freddie worked in construction with his brother Gilbert and he had an uncle who was a taxi driver. The uncle knew my mother because sometimes he picked her up in his taxi at bars and gave her a ride home. He felt sorry for me, so he got us a hotel room to stay in that night. We stayed away about a week.

My mother had never talked to me about sex at all, so I was ignorant and vulnerable at 14, feeling unloved and resented by my mother. Freddie was kind and comforting and I loved him. He was my first real boyfriend. Of course two teenagers in love together in a hotel room led to the inevitable intimacy. My mother was furious at me for running away. She called the police. I knew my brothers were probably worried about me, so one day I called home. I was scared, but I knew I had to go home. My brothers promised not to hurt Freddie, so I went home. All my family liked Freddie because he was always around running errands and fixing things around the house.

I was so young I didn't even realize I was pregnant until one day, walking to school, I had to stop and throw up. Then my monthly periods stopped, and I feared that I might be pregnant. I knew my mother would be very angry with me, so I tried to hide my stomach. One day I was going to a school dance and Mother saw me trying on dresses. She commented that I was gaining weight, saying in Spanish, "You're getting a little stomach." Mother spoke only Spanish to me. I agreed with her and said "I guess I've put on a few pounds." She didn't suspect that I was pregnant, or she would have had a fit.

I waited about five months and then I told Freddie that I had to tell my mother. He agreed, so one afternoon I saw my mother sitting in the living room and she seemed at ease. I walked up to her and said, "Mom, I have something I need to tell you."

She looked at me with a worried look, and said "What is it?"

I said "I'm pregnant, and I'm having the baby." My mother looked shocked. She looked like she was about to collapse. She said "Oh no, you can't be." She called my brothers and told them. Right away, my brother Catarino took Freddie into the other room and started beating on him. I could hear Freddie screaming. Mother was furious with me. She said, "You are going to work and take care of this baby." She looked like she hated me, but I was relieved that she wasn't going to try to make me have an abortion because I was five months pregnant. Freddie left that night for California. He was scared of my brothers. I felt abandoned by him, and I was angry. I began to hate him for leaving me alone. I knew I had to get a job and get to work. I was not going to be able to count on Freddie for anything.

6

WELCOME, LEAH ROSE

I started working in my own neighborhood. There were two elderly ladies who lived down the street from us. They were sisters and had never been married. I cleaned the house for them but mostly they just needed company. After I had cleaned, I would sit in the kitchen and have tea with them.

They were both very nice and they liked to tell me stories about their lives. Their stories were interesting and I learned a lot about the two dear old women and grew to like them a great deal.

When Halloween came, our family celebrated with a little party and gave away candy to the children who came to our door. Later in the evening, as I began to clean up the kitchen and wash dishes, I started having contractions. I didn't want to have a baby on Halloween, so I held on and tried to wait. Finally, I had to tell my mother and she called a taxi cab. My brother Catarino had been drinking and his behavior was very bad when he was drunk, and he was drunk. The cab driver refused to take us. Catarino told the driver he would take us or else he would beat him up. So there we were on the way to the

Baptist Hospital downtown: me in labor, my mother fretting, and my brother drunk.

When we arrived at the hospital, they checked me and said I was not fully dilated, so they made me walk up and down the hallway. I was in pain for a long time. I didn't give birth until the next evening at 9:25 p.m. At last, the time came, but the doctor had to do an episiotomy so the baby could be delivered. I was terrified and in pain, but at last my baby girl was born. She weighed seven and a half pounds and was twenty-one inches long. Her hair was jet black and she had dark eyes and light skin.

The doctor said she would be the next Miss America. My mother was so happy and relieved; she had been worried, but God watched over us, and my little girl was strong and healthy.

We were all thankful to God for getting the baby safely delivered, and she wasn't born on Halloween but on November 1, 1979.

A few days later I got home from the hospital, my mother gave me the news that the two elderly ladies I worked for had both died. I couldn't believe they were both gone, but after my mother explained it to me, the two elderly ladies had never been married. They lived a lifetime together. When I was in the hospital delivering the baby, one lady got sick and died, the next day the sister went to see her, at the viewing, she passed away too. I was so sad to hear the devastating news. They were two of the most remarkable elderly ladies I had ever known. I would definitely miss them.

Growing up I always felt happy and a sense of belonging. Even though I was in a large family of nine, me being third to the last I was grateful for all my brothers and sisters. I would see how hard it was for my mother having to do all the work to maintain and care for all of us. She never complained, just did everything accordingly. When she would comb my hair every morning for school, she would put my hair in a pony tail. I remember her pulling on my hair to gather it together tightly, I would always moaned because it would hurt. But she always made sure I looked as polished as possible.

I wore mostly old clothes, but they were clean, sometimes torn up, but still I was a happy child. After school a bus would pick us up and take us to a catholic church for catechism, the nuns that taught us were very strict, if we disobeyed, they would hit us on our hands with a paddle. I got hit many times because I would be chatting with the other girls.

Sometimes after getting home, my mother would let me go over my friend's house to play, but she was very careful with me. I had a neighbor named Robbie he would play with me from across the fence in the back of our house. He was very nice, he would share his toys with me. I didn't have any. But his mother would limit his play time with me and take him inside.

I used to have an old broken-down cash register I would play with, it was ragged and broken, but for me it was my prize possession. I would put rocks in it and pretend it was money. I loved that machine. And if I ever found a penny or a nickel It would fill me with such joy. I would hide them in there.

My grandmother was the next person to pass away. Her name was Lupe Carrisalez she was my mother's mother. She was from a small town, Kenedy, Texas, and she came from a very strict family. She married my grandfather Catarino Briones and had two daughters, my mother Rosa and my aunt Belen.

They were known as the two flowers because they were named after flowers.

My grandfather was also from Kenedy, Texas. My grandfather was unfaithful to my grandmother, so their marriage did not last long. My grandmother struggled to care for her girls alone.

She was catholic and her religion was very important to her until her death. Her mother would babysit from Kenedy, Texas, so my grandmother could commute to San Antonio to work. She was a very dedicated worker. She worked at the Judson Candy Company for many years. She would tell me stories of how she worked in the cotton fields at the age of nine.

The parents had taken her and her siblings out of school so they could work, because they needed them to help the family to survive financially. My grandmother told me when she would take a break, her father would offer her a cigarette. She smoked most of her life. She also drank alcohol a lot later in her later years. She had stopped drinking because her doctor advised her to. But it was too late.

She got sick and doctors found she had gangrene on her bladder. She was operated, but didn't survive. She died at the age of sixty years old. She was very kind, always helped my mother financially and when she visited us, she always gave us five dollars each. She had a Singer sewing machine and she always sewed our clothes. She never married again but she had a companion whose name was Mariano and we all called him grandpa. She was very adamant about cleanliness. When she came over our house to visit, she made us clean our house and get after my mother every time.

When my brother Joe died at the age of twenty three, she made my mother promise her they would bury her next to her first grandson Joe, and so they did. She is buried directly in front of my brother.

My brother Jesse died on August 26, 1989. We all called him Chewy, he was only 26 years old. My brother Bobby was at my house fixing some plumbing under the kitchen sink, when there was a phone call from his wife Kathy. She told him something about how they had found my brother Chewy dead. He just hung up on her, it didn't phase him. When he told me about it, I got so worried! At the time I lived fifty miles from San Antonio on my ranch. So, I told Bobby "Let's go you and me to San Antonio to find out what's happening." So, Kathy said for us to call my dad Joe. So, we both went to my dad's house. When we told him the police had told Kathy they had found my brother Chewy dead, he said "he can't be, m'ija, Chewy was here with me today drinking and playing cards."

He had gotten his income tax money and had called Betty to take the girls to see him because he wanted to give her money to buy them some clothes for school. But Betty never showed, so he was very upset. He was with a guy from school. He had been drinking Jim Bean and Coke. We were all playing cards. He left after a few hours to go see his mother, because he owed her some money and he wanted to pay her back. But somehow Chewy never made it to mom's. We then took my father to the morgue, he went in by himself and when he came back out, it was as if he had seen a ghost.

He came running out and said it is Chewy. He recognized the clothes he had on earlier. He was dead. It was awful, I was screaming and crying. I started running towards the highway to kill myself. I could not comprehend that was actually taking place right there and then. My brother Bobby ran after me and tackled me to the ground telling me "it's ok, we don't need to lose you too. Please calm down please." While my dad just looked in complete shock, none of us could believe this was happening. My brother Chewy left my dad's place with a person that we only knew had gone to school with him. We never were able to find him or locate him afterwards. There were rumors it was Sandra Villegas' brother Carlos Villegas that was with my brother Chewy. We knew them, at one time they lived with us. My mother took care of Sandra when she was pregnant and homeless. But the police refused to investigate because there were drugs involved. Supposedly, they went to get some cocaine and injected under the Grayson street, next to the golf court. I believe that guy injected my brother with an overdose to take his money. My brother Chewy went into convulsions and fell into the creek of water that was there. A passerby saw him and called EMS. My brother was dead from an accidental overdose, as the medical examiner determined. But that guy that was with him just left him there to die and took his money. I seriously believe my brother Chewy was murdered for his money. When they found him, he only had a few dollars on him. When he had gotten over two thousand dollars of income tax money. It was intentional and malice. Betty, the ex-girlfriend, had been with my brother for many years before all this. She had left my brother for an illegal alien. She had three daughters with my brother; one, she had given away at birth. My brother cared deeply for his girls and only wanted to do what was right for them. That particular day, Betty had told him she would let him see the girls and get the money, but instead stood him up. She had done this many times before. She had no regards for my brother's feelings or his good deeds. At the time of my brother's death, she was already pregnant with the other man's child. My brother loved Betty so much he had left her as his beneficiary from his job at Luby's cafeteria. She had to arrange for his funeral.

7

ADAM

It was October 26, 1995, late in the evening. We had just arrived from Michigan to San Antonio, me my ex-husband and all of my three children. We were all exhausted. Oscar had driven many long hours. I called my boyfriend Leon to let him know I was back. His tone was different, somewhat serious. He said "Mary you need to call your mom." He was adamant. So I was, ever so curious, and started to question him why. He didn't want to tell me, so suddenly he blurted out, "Your brother Adam died today." I said "Oh, no!" I quickly made arrangements to take a cab to my mother's house. As I arrived, my mother was outside on the porch with my brother Bobby. He advised me not to get my mom all wined up because he had just calmed her down. My mom started to tell me what happened. She said they were all in the kitchen eating hamburgers. It was just her, Adam and Bobby. She had been sick with the flu and Adam had been so worried for her. He had told her she needed to see a doctor and she told Adam he shouldn't worry. Adam got up and went to the bathroom. A few minutes later Bobby went into the bathroom to check on Adam because he had not come out. Adam was on the floor in a sitting position, he was not breathing, so Bobby called 911. Supposedly Adam had a seizure and fell back against the cement tub. As he fell into the sitting position, he was putting pressure on his diaphragm and could not breath. After so much time like that, Adam had died. My mother was beyond devastation. She told me she could not believe Adam was gone and she had no money for a funeral, what was she going to do? I calmed her down and assured her I would get the money together and make all the arrangements.

Adam was only twenty seven years old, his birthday was coming up in just a few days. On November 8 he would have turned twenty eight. So sad my mother's baby had died, leaving all of us in total shock and sadness. I was able to raise one thousand dollars, but the funeral director and embalmer was very understanding and worked with me. It was about six thousand dollars in total. I ended up going to work for the funeral home to pay off the remaining debt. During the rosary, my youngest son got into a fight with one of his cousins and was bleeding profusely. I had to take him to the hospital for stitches. As I walked out of the funeral home, I realized my car was gone. It had been stolen from the funeral home. My boyfriend offered to take me to the hospital. The car was a red Chrysler my ex-husband had brought all the way from Michigan for me. Now it was gone. At the time I was worried about my son getting medical attention.

The funeral was so hard, especially on our mother, and difficult on the rest of us. Adam was the baby for all the brothers. He had a pet ferret, he loved it very much. Always carried it on his shoulders; I think it kept him calm and made for less seizures. After we got home from the funeral, I went to check on the ferret and found it was dead. We had a dinner in honor of Adam and spent time reminiscing about all the memories and times we had with our little brother, and as I got back home to my house, in my bedroom the light from my lamp kept flickering on and off over and over. I started freaking out and became frightened. I called my brother Stevie to come get me to take me back to my mom's house. Years later I learned it was Adam reaching out to me to let me know he was ok. Because he knew how much I loved him and always worried about him. On November 8, 2019, I was remembering Adam on his birthday, and this is what I wrote:

Today would have been my little brother's fifty-first birthday. He was twenty seven when he passed. He was my mother's baby; she took great care of him. He had seizures most of his life. It would be a seizure

that would claim his death. I remember how he always followed me and mostly confided in me. He was

special. We would all look out for him. He loved to play scratch off tickets and drink his Dr. Peppers and diet Coke. And he liked to smoke his cigarettes. He was a big person. He did not look sick, he just had seizures at very unexpected times. My mom did not like to take him nowhere because she was scared he would have a seizure. Me and my boyfriend would take him and my mom to eat and sometimes to the movies. And we would take a chance Adam would have a seizure, we would deal with it. He was always smiling, he enjoyed it when family was all together, with his nieces and nephews. Sometimes he would get a little aggressive with my mom and she would put him in the state hospital for a few days to get treatment and then he would return home back to normal. He was smart. He got his G.E.D. He would walk to the store alone lots of times. Even if he would get a seizure, he would just get back up and

continue on his way. He loved to talk and remember events, joke around and mostly was pleasant to be around. We would all give him money for sodas, tickets and cigarettes. He loved that so much. He was like a grown up kid. My mother always made sure he had everything he needed. She was so devastated when he died. I do not think she ever got over it. Adam was her baby till his passing.

8

BOBBY

As I remember from that dreadful morning of September 11, 1998, I received a phone call from my mother, and she asked me in Spanish to please come over, that there were two detectives there at her house, they had come to inform her that my brother Bobby had been found dead. I was in total shock and overwhelmed with so much devastation. I told her I would be right over. I had two grandsons with me that I was babysitting; Steven and Anthony. I asked my ex-husband Oscar to please take me to my mother's house. Then I called my daughter Leah to pick up the kids. Oscar picked me up, I was crying hysterically, I didn't want my sons, Oscar, Nicolas and Peter to see me crying. They had been staying with their father, they all came with him to pick me up. I could not stop crying. My sons finally asked their father "why is mom crying?" And Oscar said something had happened to her brother Bobby. When I arrived at my mother's house, there were two detectives there, I asked what happened to my brother. They said they believed it was a homicide, meaning they thought my brother Bobby was killed, only they had found his body. I got very upset, I started to insist they tell me, how my brother had been killed. But they refused to say anything more.

It wasn't till the day of my brother's funeral that one of the funeral directors told me, when I asked him why my brother's hands didn't stay together, even after I put a lot of rosaries around them, that my brother Bobby had been stabbed twenty-six times. That he had fought back and had a lot of defensive wounds on both his hands. I started to cry, just imagining what they did to my brother. I was very mad. I felt I had to find out exactly what had happened. And who could do this evil and horrible act of violence to my brother, whom I loved and cared for so much. Later, there were rumors that my brother had been murdered at some bar named Rosie's, on Colorado Street and Fredericksburg road. And that his body had been taken and left on Colorado and Guadalupe Street. That's when a lady taking her child to school in the morning had come upon my brother Bobby's body. There was an elementary school across the street where my brother was found. My brother was last been seen visiting his young daughter Valerie where he had stop to leave money to his ex-girlfriend Yoli.

She lived in the projects called the Alazan courts. Supposedly, he had left to catch the bus to go home,

where he lived with my mother, only he never made it home. My brother was killed in the early

morning hours of September 11, 1998, just passed midnight. And it was more than one person involved.

That night it had rained hard, there had been thunderstorms. My brother was stabbed numerous times, one of the stab wounds went directly into his chest, which caused him to die instantly. My brother Stevie had gone to the police department before he passed away. He said they showed him pictures of when they found my brother's body, and that it was very hard to see. I cried a lot. My brother Stevie wanted to know if they had any information of who may have killed my brother Bobby. They had questioned a lot of people, but there were no leads. There were rumors that my brother Bobby owed money for drugs and that may have been the motive why they killed him, according to his ex-girlfriend Yoli. She had been interrogated for hours and denied knowing anything. A week before my brother's death, they had tried to hurt my brother at her apartment, but my brother ran out the back door. I always suspected she was directly involved, but could not prove it. My brother Bobby told me himself if anything ever happened to him it would be her. There was so much sadness surrounding the death of my brother Bobby. He was only thirty-eight years old. He left behind four children and so much confusion. All the family was left devastated. Especially my mother; he lived with her and cared for her.

That morning he left for work dressed in his white pants and shirt; he was a painter. He left and never returned. We were scared for my mother's safety. My brother Stevie made a request to the Navy for a loan so we could relocate my mom. A request like that had never been made to the Navy, so they did grant it. We were not sure if whoever killed my brother Bobby would come after my mom. My mother's heart was broken; she died four years later, on September 25, 2002. It was my brother's birthday.

I started looking like crazy to find out what had actually happened to my brother Bobby, even putting myself in harm's way, a few times they attempted to come after me. But nothing I did could bring my brother back. He left a tremendous void in my life and that of my other brothers and sister. It affected everyone in the family in different ways. There was so much anger, confusion and devastation that was overwhelming; it created a domino effect of tragic moments in our lives, of some of us that were left behind. Even in his children's lives, I'm sure. But in my heart, I truly believe my brother lives on through his daughters and son. And also, his granddaughter. They remind me so much of him. His legacy will always live on. He was an incredible person, very intelligent with a lot of love and compassion for all of his family.

9

ROSA

y mother passed away on September 25, 2002. It was the exact day of my brother Bobby's birthday. About a week earlier I had gone over to check on her. She looked swollen on her entire body, something was not right. So, I took her to the doctor as a walk-on that morning. He was her heart doctor. My mother had had a few strokes in the previous years, and also her heart rate had been elevated, so she was referred to this specialist. He was a good doctor. He saw my mom and said he would admit her into the hospital. She had too much water accumulated in her body. He said I should take her home and he would call us back as soon as there was a room available to admit her. So about three hours later they called us from the hospital, they said to bring my mother in. They were admitting her to the intensive care unit. The doctor said they just had to take some fluid out of my mom's body and she would be fine and be able to go home in a few days.

I would go every day to see my mom and help the nurses with her bathing. My mother seemed to be doing better. One day the nurses were asking her about details in case she passed away. She said, "I know I got a one-way ticket." When the nurses asked her where to, she replied laughing, "To heaven, of course." She also said if she passed, all she wanted was for everyone to gather around her and pray. And that she did not want no more poking of her body. Clearly, she did not want no autopsy. My brother Stevie and I had discussed putting my mom into a nursing home, because on certain occasions my mom had taken her medication more than once because she would forget, and that would cause her to get very sick. One time she went into a coma for a few days. But putting her in a nursing home would just be an option.

On the day before she was being released, I told my brother Stevie she was doing better, that I would keep him informed. On September 25, 2002, she was expected to be released. They had moved her to a regular room that morning. She had a friend from her housing complex that had gone to see her. That morning I spoke to her. She said my mom was very scared that morning, and insisted she take her out of the hospital because I still had not arrived and she was nervous. Her friend calmed her down and told her, "Don't worry, Mary is coming and taking you home." The nurse I talked to said she walked into my mom's room and that my mom was unresponsive. She called the doctors on shift and they pronounce my mom deceased. I think she saw the calendar on the wall right in front of her bed and that took my mom's life.

My mother had a very hard life. She endured so much abuse at the hands of my father from the moment he came into her life. He abducted her at the age of twelve from the grounds of her elementary school. She was only in fifth grade; she was not given the opportunity to learn or get an education, which she longed for. She wasn't allowed to live out her life the way she had anticipated, she was robbed of so much. Instead, she was forced to marry my dad. She was so beautiful and innocent. She was taken from her free will. Her mother was so strict and made decisions that would ultimately decide my mom's fate for her. She lived a torturous and suffering life. My father's physical and emotional abuse would persist for most of my mom's life. Even though she divorced him after twenty-five years, she loathed him with passion. And the trauma would always be there until her death. She was an incredible woman, raised all nine children basically by herself and did the best she could. She seemed nervous most of the time, she smoked a pack of cigarettes a day to help calm her down. Later in life she learned to read and write. She was very intelligent. I believe deep within my heart that my mom had so much potential if only she had been given the opportunity. She suffered a lot. My father was an alcoholic and very abusive. It was a miracle my mother didn't go insane. She was very strong. She had laid to rest four sons before her own demise. She never cried at their funerals, but they caused her heart to weaken and took years away from her life. She passed away at sixty years old.

She had numerous strokes and had been in a coma for a period of time. She finally subs come to her death suffering a heart attack on my brother Bobby's birthday. She missed my brother a lot. He lived with her and cared for her till the day he was murdered. My brother Joe shot himself in the head in the next room where my mother and father were. He killed himself at the age of twenty-three. He too could no longer endure the pain and chaos my father inflicted on him throughout his life.

His death had a tremendous effect on all of us. It was like a curse that washed itself over all of our lives.

Some kind of awful domino effect.

10

My father passed away on February 14, 2006. He had come into San Antonio to visit six months before. He called me and said he wanted me to get a small insurance on him in case he passed away someday. That way I could have enough money to cremate him and bury him. But he asked me to come in my Security uniform. He said the insurance agent would be there and he was going to talk to me about what he wanted me to do in case he died. So the day came I was going to see him at his brother Sebastian's house. So I got a hold of my sister Christina and gave her some money so she could buy stuff to make dad and my uncle a *carne quijada* dinner. When I got there, my dad gave me specific instructions I was to follow in case he passed away. He said for me to get a five-thousand-dollar insurance policy, so I could go to Reno, Nevada, to cremate him and then bury him with my mother, and then I could just keep the remaining money for me. So I sat down with the insurance agent, he was the same insurance agent my uncle had. I signed all the documents and gave him sixty dollars. I gave him all the information from my dad's doctor. My father thanked me and we all sat down and enjoyed a nice dinner. I had made rice and beans, my father complemented me on the rice and beans, he always liked my food more than my sisters'. Then my sister yelled at me and said "you better not burn dad." I told her whatever dad decides is what it's going to be.

The next day we got together with my brother Ricky, dad, my sister and me to go eat at Panchitos restaurant, that was my dad's favorite. My dad lived in Reno and there were no good Mexican places to eat there. So he enjoyed going out with us and spending quality time together. When we were going back home in Ricky's car, my sister had some documents she wanted my dad to sign. They were documents stating my dad would be responsible to pay for college courses my sister had made plans to go to. When my sister explained to my dad what the papers meant, my dad refused to sign them and told my sister he could not sign the papers because he was on a fixed income. My sister became enraged and started cussing at my dad. Said to him "you never did anything for me in my life, so the hell with you." My sister disrespecting my dad made me furious and I told my brother Ricky to stop the car and told my sister to get out. I was not going to allow that kind of disrespect for my dad. So she got out, still screaming loudly at my dad. I could tell my dad's demeaner had changed. His happy spirit just saddened him horribly. The next day my dad left back home to Reno. He was supposed to stay longer but

My sister's behavior had changed his plans.

Within a month the insurance agent sent me a letter notifying me the insurance I had gotten for my dad was not valid; they had had trouble getting information about the doctor and had sent me back a check for the sixty dollars. About a month later, I got a call from the insurance agent saying he could still get an insurance on my dad, but it was going to be much more. About one hundred and twenty dollars. So I said okay and started payments right away. So, sometime in December my dad's doctor called me to inform me my dad had leukemia, cancer of the bones. They had started chemotherapy on my dad to extend his life. I quickly decided to take a bus to go see my dad. I had spoken to him on the phone. He had told me he was fine, not to worry. He said he was eating good. He said he was eating a hamburger everyday. When I got to the hospital in Reno, I saw my dad looked sick and not himself at all. There were all kinds of food on his bed tray he had not eaten. Then I got to speak to his doctor the next day. The doctor was very blunt and told me my dad had gone to San Antonio the last time. He was supposed to inform his family and planned to move there and see another doctor in San Antonio regarding his treatment for cancer. That's when it dawned on me that's why my dad wanted the life insurance. He knew at that time about his illness, and that it was terminal and he was going to die. So I stayed a few days there with him at the hospital. I went to his apartment to clean everything so when he came out of the hospital it could be ready for him. But that did not happen. He stayed in the hospital till January receiving treatments. Then one day I received a call from the hospital; they needed to talk to me about making arrangements for my dad to leave the hospital. So I went back to Reno.

The doctors wanted to send my dad to San Antonio on a plane so he could resume medical treatments there. Then I realized my dad did not recognize me anymore. He was calling me Rosa, by my mom's name. I talked to the doctor and told him I could not take my dad to San Antonio because I had nowhere to put my dad to live. And there was no way he would get the medical bills paid like he was getting in Reno. They were paying all of his medical expenses there. But they said I had to take my dad out of the hospital that day and take him somewhere. I realized I could not take him back to his apartment. He had developed Alzheimer's disease, he could no longer take care of himself, so I made the difficult decision to put my dad in a rehabilitation facility, in other words, a nursing home there in Reno. It was the saddest and heart-breaking thing I could ever possibly do. I felt terrible, I just kept crying and hiding as I did not want my dad to see me. My dad's hair was falling out in chunks. So I called the nurse to bathe him while the ambulance got there and would transport us both to the nursing facility. I stayed there for a few hours with my dad. He looked like a lost child, I felt so sorry for him, but there was not much more I could do for him. He asked me to go get him a few sodas before I left and I left him some money in his pouch from his glasses and told him if he needed money it would be there. I don't think he understood because that money was still there when he passed.

I left the facility in tears, I could feel my heart ache so bad. The last thing he said to me was if I was coming back. I said I was, and he said to just bring him two tamales. I still had to make arrangements to empty out my dad's apartment. But I had no clue how I was going to make that happen. My dad's brother lived in Sparks, Nevada, on the outskirts of Reno, and when I talked to him, he said he would help me pay for a U-Haul truck and I could take everything to his house, and that's exactly what I did. My dad had a couple of friends that loved him across the street from my dad's apartment. They helped me to pack everything and take it all to my uncle Roy's. So, on the first of February I received a call from my dad's doctor. He said my dad had been taken back to the hospital for another set of chemo, but that his blood pressure had gone very low and he was having trouble breathing. He wanted my permission to intubate him to help him with his breathing. So my dad would be put on life support. I told the doctor to go ahead and do what was best for my father. He then said my dad had a twenty percent chance of sustaining life at this time. So I quickly made the arrangements to go to Reno. I was broke, so my ex-husband gave me some money and so did my brother Ricky. So I left on the bus back to Reno, praying my dad would still be alive when I arrive.

When I got to the hospital I saw my dad was on the breathing machine and his hands were tied up, so he wouldn't put out the tubes. He opened his eyes and was looking at me. I told him I was there and that I would not leave him. He just nodded with his head in agreement. I was crying a lot and trying my best to hide my tears from my dad, but I'm sure he could see me. He was in the intensive care unit. My dad had developed something else that was supposedly contagious. I had to suit up, just to be in the same room with him.

At my dad's apartment there was only a bed and a phone. I stayed there and would just go to be with my dad every day. It was a catholic hospital. Saint Mary's. I would go to the chapel every day and pray. Cry and beg God on my knees to guide me in the right path. What was I to do for my dad? I prayed for healing and comfort for my dad. In those days I was so confused and just took one day at a time. My dad wasn't getting better, he only weighed about eighty pounds, had no more hair, and was barely breathing. He was holding on by a thread, if anything. I kept asking God to help me to do the right thing for my father. He wasn't a good dad, and my mom and my brothers suffered because of his bad choices, but I still honored him because that's what God wanted of me.

So, on February thirteen I decided my dad had suffered enough and I made the most difficult decision to take him off life support. I called a meeting with all the doctors and nurses and told them a story about my dad. How he was always very independent and very active. How we had talked about if this ever happened, he did not want to live his life like this. The doctors had talked to me about putting a trachea in my dad's throat. That was not how my dad wanted to live. So, I decided to take him off life support that day. It was Valentine's Day. Most of the nurses were crying, I was crying, that's when the doctors said my father had left me in charge of him and that I had made the right decision under all those circumstances. I looked at my dad that morning and asked him in Spanish if he wanted me to take him off the breathing machine and if he understood he was going to die and he nodded his head in agreement, and squeezed my hand hard. So, at about one in the afternoon the nurses took off the machine. I promised my dad I would not leave him, and when it was all over, I would be the last one to walk out of that room. I told him to rest and not worry, that I would be there at his side. So, he closed his eyes for the last time and about eight in the night he took his last breath. I called the nurses to notify them my dad was gone. I looked out the window and saw it was snowing. I looked at my dad; he looked at peace and I just prayed, cried and held my dad's hand. I thanked God my dad was finally at peace.

They came and took my dad's body about midnight. It was just like I promised my dad, they wheeled him out into the elevator and I walked behind him. I had kept my promise. They told me I had until three in the afternoon to take my dad's remains out from the hospital morgue. My dad's friends picked me up from the hospital and took me to my dad's apartment that night. They gave me their condolences and left. I lay down on the hospital bed and prayed, because I had no idea how I was going to take my dad out of the morgue the next day. I had no money, only a one-way ticket back to San Antonio. When I opened my eyes I saw my dad on the ground sitting like an Indian, looking at me. I screamed. I nearly had a heart attack myself. Then I closed my eyes and he was gone. The nurses had told me that same day not to be scared if my dad came out on me because it happens when they are close to you. I never believed them till at that moment.

The next day I awoke praying and asking God for guidance. I got on the phone and called every funeral home I could. Most of them wanted money, but there was one, thank God, that said they would cremate my dad for me. I had to sign that I owed them and so forth. My dad's friends picked me up and took me to the funeral home. I signed the papers and they would take my dad's body from the hospital morgue. They asked me if I wanted to be present at the cremation and I said no. They would have the cremation done the next day. So the next morning I went to the funeral home to see my dad for the last time and pray. Then I went back to my dad's apartment and called my mom and sister to let them know what was taking place. I was feeling bad, so I just had some drinks and fell asleep. I decided to go back to San Antonio on the bus.

The next morning, they called me to go downstairs and gave me the ashes. I got on the Greyhound bus and went home. It took me three days to arrive in San Antonio. When I got home, I noticed there was a hospital bed in the living room. I asked my ex-husband Oscar what was going on. He said, "Sit down and put your dad's ashes down because there is something I need to tell you. While you were gone, I got sick and was in the hospital and the doctors decided to put me on hospice, they gave me one year to live." I was shocked beyond belief. Here I arrived exhausted and sad and in complete confusion. I didn't have any more tears to cry; my heart just felt numb. My grown-up kids were there just wanting me to cook for them, so I just went into the kitchen and began to cook to try to forget what had just occurred. Ten months later, Oscar was dead.

When I contacted the insurance agent to claim my dad's policy, I had mentioned to them that I had lost all the receipts.

Honestly, that would turn out real bad for me... The two agents came over to my house to tell me to my face that they had just put the policy in on February and that I could not prove anything because I had no receipts. I was so furious they were crooks and threw them out of my house. I still had to pay for the funeral home in Reno for my dad's cremation and needed money for my dad's funeral. My brother Catarino gave me money to open the grave to put my dad's ashes and for the priest. We had a nice funeral for my dad. I did as my dad requested and put his ashes at my mom's feet. About four months after my dad's funeral, and the insurance claim being denied, the wallet came back in the mail with all the receipts. I just had to go to the post office and show my identification. I then called the corporate headquarters for the insurance company and explained about the agents denying the claim. Now I had all the receipts. They told me to send copies of all the receipts, so I did. Then about a week later I received a letter from the corporate. They said they just wanted me to answer one question. When did I find out my dad's illness was terminal? I was happy to answer them. I sent them the doctor's information and phone number. And within a month, they sent me a check for five thousand dollars. I was able to go to Reno and pay the funeral home what I owed.

11

CHRISTINA

It was June 26th, 2009. I had dinner with a friend that evening. It was so pleasant. Then at about one in the morning I was awakened by the phone ringing. When I answered it, it was a man who said he was calling from the Henderson prison. He said my sister Christina Cervantes had put my name as next of kin. He said my sister was on the way to the hospital by ambulance, she had gone into a seizure. I asked him for his name and the name of the hospital my sister had been taken to. By this time, I was crying and pretty shaken up. I didn't quite know what to do, so I called my brother Catarino and told him what was going on. He could tell I was crying hysterically, but told me he was out of town. The best thing I could do was call our brother Stevie, who was in Dallas, Texas. He was closer to Henderson, Texas. So I called my brother Stevie and explained the situation to him. He told me to calm down and not to worry. He would go to the hospital and be with our sister.

He called me when he got to the hospital, after finding out exactly what was going on. He said that the doctors had intubated my sister to stabilize her. He said they told him my sister had gone into convulsions at the minimum-security prison, and when she arrived at the hospital she wasn't breathing. So they put her on a breathing machine. He said the doctors said my sister was brain dead. And so, my brother pleaded with the doctors to please run some more tests on my sister, to make sure she was in fact brain dead. I had already called my work to let them know I wasn't coming in because of the situation with my sister. Then my brother called and said he had overheard the guards saying my sister had stopped breathing at the prison and there were no one there that knew CPR, so my sister had no one perform CPR on her when she stopped breathing. So, when the doctors told my brother my sister was indeed brain dead, my brother made the difficult decision to take my sister off the ventilator, that was the only thing keeping her alive. My brother Stevie said he told my sister not to worry about the kids, that he would take good care of them. He told her to go ahead and rest, that's when he saw tears streaming down my sister's face. And at about one in the afternoon my sister took her last breath.

My brother said that as soon as the nurses saw my sister had passed away, they told him to leave because it was now a crime scene. My brother became angry and asked them what is happening here, my sister didn't kill no one, she had problems with alcohol and drugs. They still made him leave or threatened to call Security to escort him out.

My brother called me to tell me my sister had passed away about one in the afternoon. I just got so sad and cried. It was my birthday and I would never forget this dreadful day. After all that, my brother called the prison and demanded answers. No one wanted to cooperate with us. I called the prison to notify them about my sister's funeral arrangements and they rudely told me my sister was property of the Huntsville prison system and that she would be buried in Huntsville, Texas. I told them that I would not allow it and if I had to call the governor of Texas, I would. And that I needed to find out what exactly occurred on the night of June 25th, when my sister went into convulsions there at the prison. There were cameras inside the room my sister was in, so there had to be a video of what had actually happened. But no one wanted to talk to me or my brother. I had written letters to a lot of important people regarding the situation with my sister. So, it wasn't till a month later when we were able to get my sister's body to San Antonio. They had taken her body to Galveston, Texas, for an autopsy. She actually died in Tyler, Texas, because they had taken her from a hospital in Henderson, Texas, to a trauma specialty hospital in Tyler, Texas. We had decided with Rodriquez funeral home. The funeral home only allowed the immediate family to view my sister for an hour. Her body had been deteriorated and we had to cremate her.

The day of the viewing was such an emotional day for all my family. I cried so much. I could not believe my little sister was gone at the age of forty years old. She had four sons and a daughter. Three sons were already older, except for her nine-year-old son, whom my daughter had adopted. I had to tell him of his mother's death, which was the saddest thing I could ever do. She had another son and a daughter that had been taken away when they were born due to my sister's drug abuse. But I was determined to find out what had happened to my sister. I started to write letters to everyone I could think could help me. No, my little sister was a good-hearted person. Yes, she had problems with alcohol, but no one could do anything because she was in the custody of the state of Texas. My sister was a good-hearted person. She had problems with alcohol and drugs, but mostly it stemmed from all the tragic events in her life. It was ultimately a tumor in her bladder that caused her early death.

12

STEVE

I t was on a Wednesday, January 15th, 2015. I received a call from my Deacon in Tyler, Texas. I was working down-town at a Via Metropolitan information center. My phone rang so I ran into the restroom, because we were not allowed to be on the phone while on duty. When I answered the phone, a man asked me if I knew Steve Cervantes and I said "yes, sir, that's my brother." And he said "I'm so sorry to tell you this, but he passed away on Monday morning." He said he'd tried calling other numbers from his wallet, but no one answered until he called me. I started to cry. All of this was so unex-pected. The man just kept on saying "I'm sorry, I'm sorry." I asked him to give me his name and the name of the hospital because I had to notify my brother's children and then get back to him.

I immediately called my boss and explained to him what had happened, as I needed to go home. He said he understood and made arrangements for someone to relieve me of my duties. I then called my other brother, Catarino, to tell him about the call, but I was crying hysterically. He said he would call me back. When he called me back, he asked if I could talk and I said yes. He said Aunt Belen had just called and said they called and said our brother Stevie had died. I said it was me that called, and he said "Oh, you sounded like Aunt Belen." Then my son Oscar overheard my brother on the phone and told me he would get a hold of my niece Lori, and he would go pick me up because he had my car. When my son picked me up I went to the bank and withdrew some money. I then called my niece Lori; she was at work. She asked if she needed to leave work. I said yes, this is important, so we made plans to meet at a restaurant. She got there with her little brother Stevie and her step sister Star and I told him what the Deacon had said. They seemed sad and started to cry, but my brother's son just seemed sad. They said what do we do now; I said we need to call the funeral home to make funeral arrangements.

About a year and a half before my brother Stevie passed away, his girlfriend Madi had called me to tell me she was taking my brother to the hospital because he was bleeding out from all the veins in his neck; they had detached themselves due to the heavy drinking my brother was doing. I also talked to my brother who seemed very hyper and overly anxious. He said he was going to the hospital or this time he wasn't coming out. Madi had called an ambulance. She was so scared when she saw my brother throwing up so much blood. The doctor said that it saved my brother's life getting him to the hospital so quickly. Then, the next day Madi called to say my brother was in intensive care and had a breathing machine that was breathing for him.

The next day, my niece Lori, my nephew little Stevie and my ex-sister-in-law Angie went to see my brother in the hospital in Tyler, Texas. They took me with them. He was unconscious, but the following day he was talking. The breathing machine was off of him. I went into his room and he asked me to pray for him, which I did. I placed my hand on his head. His girlfriend Madi was with him and she did not like the idea that my brother's ex was there, but my brother survived and went into rehab for about 9 months. But a year later he called to tell me a unique and extraordinary story: he said the day that he was bleeding out, as he laid there on the pavement waiting for EMS, he saw this bright white light. It was round and it came into his hand. He said it felt like the most incredible feeling of peace and a serene loving feeling. He said that at that point he was ready to die because the feeling he got was so overwhelming and glorious he didn't want it to go away. He said he would never forget that as long as he lived.

My brother Stevie had joined the Navy when he was 18 years old. He was working in construction and he had gotten off work. As he walked home tired and all dirty, he said he passed a recruiting office, and that's when he decided to apply for the Navy. He had been in the Navy for 30 years when he retired. He was very proud of all his achievements. He was a Chief in the Navy and he had all kinds of medals. He was actually shot in the leg in one of his secret assignments overseas. He never told no one until he retired he had his own business where he sold military memorabilia: caps, military shirts, military medals and all pertaining to the military. He called it Chief's Mess. He had a daughter and his son with his first wife, his step daughter, and also had a daughter in New Mexico, with a second wife, and a son with his ex-girlfriend in Houston.

Many feelings of dread and hurt about the death of my brother Steve. Many unanswered questions still boggle my mind. I do not know why his children are acting so strange. I know it is difficult for them too, but his sadness and pain... I feel there should be a boundary where we should reach out to one another and I realize everyone mourns in their own way. I just cannot cease to stop the emptiness, it lingers like a bad odor in the air. Will it ever go away? Maybe in time it will unravel death befalls me once again. How will this pattern stop? I often ask God why he left me behind; what is his purpose? What is ultimately his plan? When will it be clear to me? The realization of it all be my awakening. I know life is short and I see how life is unveiling in the life of my children and grandchildren and sadness fills me every time. Have I been such a bad mother, and if I failed to see it, how could I have been so blind? I pray to God to make me see so I can make peace with all my children before I exit this world. I want to love them and show them how much I truly love them. I want to spend time with my grandkids too, and God willing, I can make my dream come true and publish this book and tell the Story of My Life. Every time someone in my family dies, all kinds of things cross my mind. I wonder about the afterlife and how it was for my loved ones to have left this Earth. What was the last thing that went through their minds. Were angels truly there to guide them to the other side? Were my father's and mother's brothers and sister there to greet them with open arms, to take him to our Savior? God has really blessed me so much I cannot even complain. God is good to me and I am grateful to my lord for keeping me sane through all these tragic times and for forgiving me for all I have done to dishonor him. Please, Father God, forgive me for I'm not worthy of your forgiveness, and I know how much you love me. Grant me the courage to ask forgiveness of my children. Father, let me live my life in accordance to you. Have mercy for me, my God. Thank you for allowing me to live, to be here for my brothers and sister, as I know they all needed me so much.

13

OSCAR

Well, I was going to high school. I would go half a day, then go home and change clothes so I could go work at Luby's Cafeteria till 10:00 at night. I had a neighbor across the street; her name was Nena and her two daughters lived there with her. Both of them had a couple of children and she had a brother named Oscar who sometimes stayed there. When I walked home from the school it was about 2 blocks away. Oscar had a friend named Eddie and every time I passed by, Eddie would flirt with me, whistle at me, and I would always ignore him. He annoyed me so much. One time I threw a rock at him because he was getting too close to me. So one day Eddie made a bet with Oscar; he told Oscar to flirt with me and see if I would respond. So one day, as I was passing by, Oscar waved at me and I smiled and I figured if I waved back and smiled he would think I liked Oscar and would leave me alone. Little did I know Oscar would become the love of my life and we would be married, so one day school had ended and on one evening I was walking to the nearby store to buy Leah Rose some ice cream. When I got out of the store, Oscar was outside standing beside his car and he called me to come over. So I did. He asked me how I was doing and how old was my daughter, and I told him she was two and a half. He said if I wanted a ride home, so I was trying to be polite and I said yes, and we got home.

I was carrying my daughter in my arms and Oscar said "Why do you carry her, can't she walk?" I said "Yes, she can walk, she just likes for me to carry her. I don't see her very much. I often work and go to school. My mother takes care of her for me...," So we started talking, I went and left Leah Rose with my mom and went back across the street to talk to Oscar. He was very handsome and charming; he had dark hair and light skin, very glossy black eyes, and he was flirting with me. I asked him how old he was, he said he was 42 and I said you're too old for me. He smiled and said "Try it, you might like it." I just laughed and we would talk and see each other occasionally. He would always ask if I needed to go to the store shopping. If he was around, he would take me and he was very nice. One day in the evening we were hanging around outside and he asked me what is it that you want from life right now. I said I want to finish school. I was only 17. I wanted to buy my mama a house then I wanted to get a car, so he said "Do you have money saved to get your mama a house?" And I said my mother has about $1,000 save to put down for the house and she's saving every day, so Oscar said "My nephew Arthur is a real estate agent and broker, he can get your mother a house, and I'll talk to him so he can talk to your mom," and that made me start trusting Oscar.

I had never met anyone like him. He was so sure of himself and he made all things seem so easy. There was something about him that made me want to be around him. He was addictive. The following week, Arthur, Oscar's nephew, found my mother a house on the west side of town and I was so happy. We were going to move in the next month. We didn't have to rent anymore. The house was perfect; it was big. It had three apartments in it, my mother would live in one and the others would be rented out. All she had to do was collect the rent and the place would end up paying for itself. We moved in. My mother and me, my brother Jesse with his wife Betty, his two girls, and my brother Catarino. I started seeing Oscar every time I had a chance. He worked out of town, he ran a cotton gin and Mathis, Texas, and he would mostly come on the weekends. He would take me to eat, to the movies and we would just hang out, and that summer, on June 26th, it was going to be my birthday and I had plans to spend it with Oscar. Well, the day came and my mother was upset with me. She wanted to have a little party for me at home with the family, so I told her that I was already going to spend time with Oscar. She didn't like it at all; she said you can go, but you're not taking the baby with you. I went to see Oscar that day. He wanted to give me something, but all he had was his gold ring with the little diamond on it. It was a man's ring, but he put it on me. It felt perfect and I was so delighted, that made my day special.

I was becoming more and more comfortable with Oscar. Every time I was with him, he made all of my problems fade away and I never felt so good. I just couldn't be away from him; I would even take the trailway bus on weekends to go see him in Mathis, Texas. He would take care of us. He was so thoughtful and respectful, and yet so loving. I was falling in love with him and I would get butterflies in my stomach every time I laid my eyes on him. Then one weekend I was at home and my mother wanted to talk to me about Oscar. She said he was too old for me. She was upset that I was seeing him, and so she said "If you don't stop seeing him, you have to go." She was mad hollering, so I grabbed my daughter to get ready to go and my mother said "You can go, but you aren't taking the baby."

So I grabbed my things and my daughter and I rushed out the door. I didn't even get a chance to get her shoes. I left. I was crying and I called Oscar from the pay phone. He said he would come and get me. He said don't worry about the shoes. He got Leah Rose some pretty sandals and we went to the movies. It was great again. He had a talk with his sister Nena and asked if I could stay with her and Leah Rose. He said he would pay her to babysit when I went to work. He would be out of town and he would leave me his car, so I could go to work. Everything was good, but Nena's house was so hot, and I was sleeping on the sofa with the fan on me, and Leah Rose, and there was this big piano in the living room and at night mice would come out of it. I couldn't sleep, I was scared for my daughter.

Two weeks later, I told Oscar about it. Then, when he came home, he said he was getting an apartment for me and my daughter, and he did. He continued working out of town. It was summer and he would come to see us on the weekends. The only thing he wanted was for me to stay at home and take care of my Leah Rose. He didn't want me to work anymore, so I did as he said. I was very happy spending time with my daughter. I didn't know how to be a mother, but I had to adapt a lot. About a month later, he asked if I wanted to marry him. He did not want to violate me any way. He said he loved me. Again, he didn't want to violate me in any way; he said he loved me. We had a lot of years in between us. He was a lot older, I was 18 years old and I told him I would marry him. I couldn't imagine my life without him. The only problem I had was that I had to go get my birth certificate at my mother's house, so I went to my mother's house and I told her I needed to get some of my things. She didn't know what. Two weeks later we were married. It was the happiest day of my life.

I did not tell my parents till two weeks later. I knew they were against it, but I thought I was old enough to make that decision, and I did. I promised my little girl I would get her a good daddy, and I did. We went to the courthouse and got everything in order and got married on August 16th, 1982. We dressed in the best clothes we had and we went to the San Francisco Steakhouse. It was so luxurious. Ladies would swing on the stage, they had hot bread and cheese at the tables, it was so wonderful I was on top of the world. And so was Oscar. I never felt so loved and special in my whole life. I had married the man of my dreams.

After a month of being married, I got pregnant with my first son Peter. I started to be seen by an Indian doctor named Dr. Bhatia. She took Incredibly good care of me. When I reached my ninth month and still had not gone into labor, the doctor decided to induce me, which meant she would put a machine attached to my stomach, in which the pains would be induced and I would go into labor. So, early in the morning of July 15, 1983, I went to the hospital and the procedure began. My son Peter was born at 2:05 in the afternoon. During the delivery I began to hemorrhage and lost a lot of blood. The doctor told Oscar I would need a blood transfusion, and he needed to sign to give them permission, but Oscar was concerned about AIDS and refused to sign. He said he had faith that I would be okay. I endured a lot of pain; the doctor had to stitch me up without anesthesia and. with God's help, I survived. The baby weighed seven and a half pounds. That's why, I think, I had those complications. Although I felt like I almost died, my son was born healthy. When I first held him in my arms, he was so beautiful it was like I was holding a live doll. Never had I seen such a beautiful child. I was so proud and filled with immense joy. Nothing in the world could compare to that joyous moment in time. When Leah Rose came to the hospital with Oscar, and she saw me with the baby in my arms, she was upset and started to cry. I told her she now had a little brother to play with. She was so used to being the only child and we spoiled her a lot, so I guess it was normal.

Oscar and I lived in a small apartment, and he worked for the telephone company, which meant he traveled a lot and was on the road a lot. So, I spent a lot of time with the kids alone and learned to be a mother for them. Peter was born on Oscar's birthday, only the year in reverse. Oscar was born in 1938 and Peter was born in 1983. That was just so awesome to me. A year later, I got pregnant again. But this time, I was constantly in pain. The doctor would give me injections on a regular basis, so I could hold onto the baby. But after a few months of complications, it became too much and I lost the baby. It was a boy. I was so devastated and got really depressed. I cried a lot and prayed all the time for strength, because I had to care for my other children. Oscar was very supportive, but it was a very hard time for me, one I would never forget. After a year in the apartment, Oscar moved us to a property with fifteen acres in the hill country, fifty miles away from San Antonio. We lived in a trailer. It was perfect for the whole family, a lot of space for the kids to play. We had nine cats, two dogs, two rabbits, three female goats and an old billy goat. Oscar had all kinds of jobs that kept him on the road a lot, so the times we spent together were cherished.

After two years I asked Oscar for another baby, but he was hesitant. I was ever so persistent, and he finally agreed. This time the doctor took extra care of me because I developed gestational diabetes. So, I was put on a very strict diet and was hospitalized for about a week. It was a good pregnancy. Only thing, we live so far away... fifty miles from San Antonio. So, the doctor thought it would be best to induce the baby. So, on February 11, I went to the hospital early in the morning. I was supposed to be there by seven, but I started going into labor at about six in the morning. On the way I told Oscar and he started to speed down the highway. He thought I was having the baby in the truck. We made it to the hospital and, thank God, my doctor was there and delivered the baby an hour later, at eight in that morning. It was a smooth delivery. The baby weighed only six pounds. He was tiny, he would fit in a shoe box. Oscar was afraid to carry him in fear he may slip out of his arms. He called the baby his little rat. In Spanish, he called him his little "Ratita." Oscar picked us up at the hospital on Valentines' Day. I had the baby in one arm and a dozen roses on the other. I was so happy to finally have my little family complete.

We lived in the ranch for about eight years. It was always so cold there. Every year it would snow. Oscar ended up getting sick, he got asthma and one time he developed ulcers and he almost died on me. One morning I had taken the kids to catch the bus down the street. When I went into the kitchen, I saw a lot of blood in the trash can. Oscar was throwing up blood. When I asked him about it, he denied it. I got so scared I call an ambulance and he was transported to a hospital in San Antonio. He kept throwing up blood. He had to have several blood transfusions. The doctors said I saved his life by getting him to the hospital on time. He finally recovered. But he developed COPD , which is like a cancer of the lungs. We moved to San Antonio and bought an old house. I had to go to school to get my medical assistant certificate so I could work. Oscar got on disability. He cared for the kids while I worked. A year later, our house burned down due to old wiring which caught on fire with lightning. Thank God we were not home. Oscar and I had gone on a small vacation. So much devastation.

This started causing problems with our marriage, and a year later we got divorced. But we remained close because of Oscar's sickness. I ended up taking care of Oscar till his death, fifteen years later. The years were very challenging, enduring so many hardships. Those of my brothers and sister and that of Oscar, my mother and my father. My journey was guided by God alone. Many times I did not know what to do or where to turn. But deep in my heart, I knew God Of The Valley was leading the way.